FROM IRON BUTT TO
MELTED HEART

MARSHALL MADILL

ISBN 978-1-0980-9710-3 (paperback)
ISBN 978-1-0980-9711-0 (digital)

Christian Faith Publishing, Inc.
832 Park Avenue
Meadville, PA 16335
www.christianfaithpublishing.com

Printed in the United States of America

FOREWORD

I first met Marshall at our local Christian Motorcycle Association (CMA) meeting in Topeka, Kansas. We joined the organization at about the same time, looking for a way to serve Jesus and to ride with fellow Christians. Marshall and I developed a good working relationship and close friendship during those early days serving in CMA.

Marshall is a type A personality, and when he sets his mind on something, it's not a question of if he will get it done, only when. So when Marshall came up with any big new idea, I simply asked how I could help because I knew it was going to happen.

This leads up to Marshall and his "48 plus one" ride. Marshall first came to me with this idea to ride through forty-eight states plus Alaska in ten days. I love riding motorcycles and enjoy life on two wheels, but this sounded like more work than enjoyment. God wasn't giving any of Marshall's close friends and riding companions the desire to join him on this ride. That is because God had a plan, and He only had Marshall going on this adventure.

As you read how Marshall went from an iron butt to a melted heart, you will see that God was determined to change a heart and let some of His children know He loved them. The "48 plus one" was to be more about glorifying God and sharing His love than anything else.

This book is a wonderful account of how grace, love, and determination all worked together to accomplish a dream. A life-changing adventure from start to finish. The Marshall I met in early 2011 is not the man I know now.

I'm proud and blessed to call Marshall my friend and brother in Christ. I believe with all my heart that after reading this book, you will be encouraged to pray harder and to dream bigger, praying God will also use you in a mighty way.

Now put your boots, gloves, and helmet on. Then ride along with Marshall as he goes from iron butt to melted heart.

Mike McClain

Area Rep, CMA, KS

Introduction

I arrived back in Topeka, Kansas, on July 7, 2016, on day 14 of an "Iron Butt" motorcycle ride that had taken me through all forty-eight lower United States plus Alaska covering over eleven thousand miles. I had just completed the epic journey on my motorcycle under the rules set forth by the Iron Butt Association called "48 States Plus Alaska."

I have commented many times since the ride that I wish I had a dollar for every person that asked me, "How's your butt?" I have also been asked repeatedly if I had fun. This is the story of my adventure that I was certain would test the limits of my physical endurance, or at least my butt, and while I didn't have time to have much fun along the way, it was an experience that I will treasure for the rest of my life.

What started out as merely a "bucket list" experience turned into at least sixty encounters with individuals from all over the world. I am convinced that I did not meet these people by coincidence but that each one of these encounters were truly divine appointments.

This is the story of how God chose to allow me to have an incredible "bucket list" experience that began with absolutely no consideration of how God would be involved and gradually opened my eyes and my heart to how He could be a part of the adventure.

By the time I arrived back home, it was not about how my butt was; it was about what had happened to my heart. I watched God use me from the very beginning of the trip to the end and beyond. I don't know that anyone could experience what I did without being changed. Please come along with me as I relive this journey and show you how God took me from Iron Butt to Melted Heart.

CHAPTER 1
A BLESSED REUNION

It was about 9:00 a.m. on Thursday, July 7, 2016. I was stopped at a gas pump about an hour north of Omaha, Nebraska, just off I-29. This wasn't exactly the middle of nowhere, but this gas station had only pay-at-the-pump. No convenience store or even a bathroom.

But the lack of convenience was the least of my concern as I impatiently filled my Harley-Davidson Road King fuel tank. I could tell from the Life360 App on my cell phone that my wife, Jan, and two of our close friends from Christian Motorcyclists Association were sitting less than a mile away from me back out on I-29.

Jan, Mike McClain, and Chuck Bramhall had left home in the dark early morning hours in the midst of a ridiculous thunderstorm that took trees down as far north as Auburn, Nebraska. They wanted to join me for the final leg of the ride I was about to complete. They wanted to be a part of the ride that had taken nearly fourteen days and covered over 11,300 miles.

I had not seen my wife in over a week. Even though I had discovered a few minutes earlier that Jan was coming to meet me, when the realization that she was so close hit me, I could hardly contain my excitement. I knew they were tracking me with the same app that I was tracking them. Why are they stopping back out on the interstate instead of coming on down to the station? Oh well, it doesn't take long to fill up a motorcycle gas tank. I replaced the cap and headed back toward the on ramp. I could see the motorcycles long before I could see the riders. Then, there they were.

I pulled up alongside their bikes, took my helmet off so I could kiss my wife, and then just sat there blubbering like a baby. I was not at all expecting, nor prepared for, the wave of emotions that poured over me in that reunion on I-29. The trip of a lifetime, which was nearly a year and a half in the planning, had finally been completed, except for the celebratory ride with my wife and friends on back to Topeka.

Jan had ridden with me from Topeka to Idabel, Oklahoma, thirteen days earlier. Idabel was the official starting line for the "48 States Plus Alaska" Iron Butt motorcycle endurance ride. Now she had braved incredibly horrible weather so she could ride with me again the final miles of the adventure. There is no way I could have ever even attempted this trip without the complete support of my wife. I never really appreciated how supportive she was until I saw her there on the on ramp. Then when I found out about the weather...

Over the fourteen days on the road I encountered my own share of crazy weather. Over one-hundred-degree heat the first couple of days and forty-five-degree cold and rain in Canada. I felt like my motorcycle was going to be blown right out from under me in the mountains of western Arizona. I nearly got washed off the road by a flash flood just north of Needles, California, where they say it never rains.

But I also saw literally every contiguous state of these amazing United States of America, from sea to shining sea. I met someone in every single state and shared the love of Jesus Christ with them. To at least one person in each state I was able to give a New Testament Bible from CMA called "Hope for the Highway."

The people I met along the way were truly inspiring, each in their own way. I was only rejected by one man over the entire trip. I was able to actually pray with many of the ones that received the Bible. I am still communicating with one of the recipients even today.

What began as purely a selfish desire on my part to show everyone how tough I am, and maybe prove to myself that I still have it at nearly sixty years old, turned into a life-changing, heart-melting experience. From the final weeks before the ride to the initial moments of the actual ride, to the reunion on I-29, and even beyond the official end of the ride through telling the story over and over again, God's handprints were definitely all over the experience.

In the chapters that follow, I will try to help you experience some of the awe and wonder that I was so blessed to witness first-hand. I will also introduce you to some of the amazing people I met along the way. I am forever grateful that God not only provided me the opportunity to experience this adventure, but He also saw fit to use someone like me in such a mighty way. Please come along with me as I relive "48 States Plus Alaska"—Iron Butt style.

CHAPTER 2
WHAT IN THE WORLD ARE YOU THINKING?

The first thoughts of riding my motorcycle to Alaska were planted in my mind when I was a teenager growing up in Chanute, Kansas. Our local newspaper had a story about a local resident that had ridden his motorcycle to Alaska. I immediately decided that someday, I was going to do the same thing.

At that time I was riding a 1972 Suzuki GT500. I rode with three guys that also made up a gospel quartet that we were all a part of. We called ourselves "The Minutemen." It was back in the days leading up to the bicentennial celebration for our great country, and we were thinking of the important role the soldiers called "Minutemen" played in the Revolutionary War and how the United States of America would probably not even exist without the "Minutemen." We also testified to the fact that we were "ready to witness for the Lord in a minute"!

The other three guys were older than me. They all had full-time jobs and way more income than I did as a high school and then college student. That also meant that they had way better motorcycles than I did. That's not a putdown on my Suzuki; it's just a statement that they were able to purchase much bigger and better motorcycles than I could afford. Still, we rode all over the place, and I loved every mile of it.

As I continued to think about Alaska, I imagined I would pull a trailer behind my motorcycle with all the gear I would need to camp all along the trip. I was also figuring it would take a total of a month for the round trip. Since it would require a month, and I had never taken more than a week of vacation at one time, I had resigned to the fact that this was never going to happen until I retired.

During the years of raising our children, I didn't even own a motorcycle, so the dream was far back in my consciousness. But I can honestly say that it never died. I told numerous people that one of my very top bucket list dreams was to ride my motorcycle to Alaska.

Finally, in 2007, with the youngest child just graduating from college and Jan and me suddenly becoming empty nesters, we got a motorcycle. Then, in the spring of 2008, we got a second bike so we could each ride our own. We immediately began taking trips on the bikes and loving every mile of it. We even joined the Christian Motorcyclists Association (CMA) so we could ride with fellow Christians and discovered an entirely new family of fellow believers and motorcycle enthusiasts.

Over the years, I had also read about these riders called Iron Butts. To qualify as an Iron Butt, you have to ride your bike one thousand miles in a twenty-four-hour period. Jan and I were thinking we were doing well when we did four hundred miles in a day. I remember thinking there is no way I could do one thousand miles in one day.

That notion was confirmed in 2012 when Jan and I rode our bikes to Dayton, Ohio. Our oldest son was living in Dayton at the time, and all the kids were converging on Dayton for the Labor Day Holiday weekend. It was seven hundred miles each way, which we did in a straight shot both going out and coming home. I remember being *totally* exhausted when we got home. We could barely walk, but we didn't want to sit down either, so we were in a real mess. Again, I declared that there is no way I could ever ride one thousand miles in a day.

So while I had long dreamed of riding my motorcycle to Alaska, I had absolutely no aspirations of being an Iron Butt. Then on April 10, 2015, at a visitation for my brother in Christ and fellow CMA'er Daryl Oglesby's father, who had passed away on Easter Sunday, several CMA friends were talking about Iron Butt rides. Lo and behold, I discovered several people I knew were actually very much into Iron Butt riding. Then someone mentioned the ultimate Iron Butt ride was 48 States Plus Alaska in ten days or less.

Something inside me stirred when I heard *Alaska*. Even though I had been quite certain that I would never be able to ride one thousand miles in a day; if these friends of mine could do it, I was now quite certain that I could do it too. I pretty much made my mind up to do 48 States Plus Alaska standing right there in the sanctuary of Community Revival Center Church in Ottawa, Kansas, on that Friday evening in 2015.

I went home and googled 48 States Plus Alaska and found a website with lots of information including rules and several suggested routes. Being from Kansas, the obvious choice for me was the route that started in Idabel, Oklahoma. I spent several tedious hours transposing the route from an internet picture to an atlas and figuring out exactly what highways I would be traveling.

Even though, in the beginning, I was not at all interested in certifying the ride, I studied the rules carefully and committed to following the rules exactly. Thus began hours upon hours of studying the route and trying to memorize every highway and every change from one highway to another.

I studied my calendar and determined the dates for the trip. In order to take advantage of the longest days of the year and also include a holiday so I would miss less time from work, I chose to start the official ride on Saturday, June 25, 2016. That still gave more than a year to prepare.

I also needed to prove to myself that I could actually ride my motorcycle one thousand miles in a day. I scheduled my first one-thousand-mile ride for Saturday, June 13, 2015. I would ride to Dallas and back. But as the day approached, I knew that just doing one one-thousand-mile day didn't really prove anything in light of what I was planning to do. So I scheduled for the very next day to ride up to Albert Lee, Minnesota, over to Sioux Falls, South Dakota, and then back down I-29 to home. That would give me back-to-back one-thousand-mile days and give me a pretty good indicator of whether or not I could actually pull this off.

My good friend Joe Rogers had also never done one thousand in a day, and he decided to go with me on the Saturday ride to Dallas. We pulled out at 5:00 a.m. in a steady rain. The rain was off and on until we got to the north part of the Dallas Metroplex. It was just after noon by then. The clouds broke, and sun was suddenly baking us. We were in traffic and had no way of getting our rain gear off. We were both sweating so bad we were having trouble keeping our eyes open. We decided to just get off at the next exit we came to so we could get out of our steamy rain gear and cool off. That shortened our ride by about three miles. Oh well.

We grabbed a sandwich and a drink and headed back north. Now the sky was almost clear. The sun was beating down on us, but once we were rolling, it was perfect riding weather. We were just back into Southern Oklahoma when we started seeing dark, ominous clouds up ahead and to the west. We thought we might get lucky and get past the system before it got to the highway. No such luck. It was about 3:30 p.m. according to my clock, but it looked like midnight. The wind was blowing so hard it felt like it was going to blow us right off the road. Thankfully, we only had to deal with that storm for about ten minutes. It was gone just as fast as it had arrived.

My odometer said we had traveled seven hundred miles. We were just north of Oklahoma City. We had been on the road twelve hours by then. My body ached all over. My brain was rebelling. We pulled into a convenience store, mainly just to allow us to get off the bikes for a while. At that point, I really didn't think I was going to be able to do this thing. I was feeling extremely defeated. Of course, I also knew that I had to get home, so we gingerly crawled back on our bikes. Once we got headed north again, and especially once I crossed back into Kansas, it was like I got a second wind, and the last 175 miles home was a breeze.

I got up and rolled out just before 5:00 a.m. the next morning (just a little over six hours after I got home from Dallas) and headed north to Minnesota. I made it to Albert Lee well before noon and was still feeling great. It was midafternoon when I got over to Sioux Falls, and I was so far ahead of the pace from the day before my attitude was soaring. Even though I rode about thirty miles further on day two, I was home nearly an hour earlier than I got home on day 1. It turned out that the second day was actually easier than the first day had been. That let me know that this was going to be more of a mental challenge than physical.

Through the rest of the 2015 riding season, I did several more long rides and continued to study, study, study the route that I had now fully mapped. I rowed and rowed and rowed on my rowing machine to help strengthen my core and toughen up my butt. I was doing everything I knew to do to prepare myself both physically and mentally for this epic adventure to which I was now fully committed.

Early in 2016, as I continued to plan and study and prepare for the 48 Plus Ride, as I had now begun to refer to it, the Lord started speaking to my heart. He laid the question on my heart, asking me why I was so willing to commit hours and hours to planning, studying, and preparing for a little ole motorcycle ride that was going to last all of fourteen days if all goes as planned.

Why indeed was I so wrapped up in this motorcycle ride which, up to this point, had been purely a selfish desire on my part to check off a line on my bucket list, when I spend so little time seeking guidance from the ultimate source of direction for the rest of my life?

I knew the Lord was not asking me to give up the trip; He just wanted me to not only take Him with me, but let Him lead the way. I asked Him how He wanted to use this trip. He reminded me of the rules for the trip, especially the one which stated that I had to stop in each state and buy something in order to get a receipt with the address, date, and time of purchase printed on the receipt. The Lord was telling me, since I had to make these certification stops anyway, why don't I look for someone that I can talk to at each stop? The Lord was telling me, "Just tell them I love them."

From that conversation with Jesus, I was inspired to give away a "Hope for the Highway" as a way to connect with the people I talked to. I then decided to write a letter to place inside the Bible just in case someone opened the Bible long after I was gone from the scene.

Skip and Benda Courtois, friends of ours from both our church and CMA, wanted to purchase a case of Bibles for me to take. Since there are fifty in a case, I was set. Another friend from church, Dave Parry, had just purchased a bunch of DVD copies of the Jesus Film. He offered to give me fifty copies to take with me. I thought it was a great idea, but I also knew there was no way I had enough room to carry the DVDs with me on the bike. Instead I got ahold of fifty business card-sized directions for downloading the Jesus Film app onto your smartphone. I was able to place one of these cards in each Bible along with the letter.

I was able share the plans for the ride with dozens of our CMA friends and our entire church family. I was also able to share in several churches before the ride. Each time I spoke about the ride, I shared the calling the Lord had given me to tell the people that He loves them. Each time I shared this, I asked for prayer. Prayer for me and Jan during the ride, but more importantly, prayer for the people that I was going to meet along the way. I asked for discernment to know exactly the person the Lord wanted me to share with each time I stopped. I asked for wisdom to know the words the Lord would have me share.

As the day for departure got closer and closer, and the call from the Lord for me to surrender this trip to His guidance became clearer and cleared, I was both overwhelmed and intimidated. I could not read the letter to anyone without crying. The sense of responsibility for the people I was about to meet was incredible.

I later realized I was still trying to do this trip in my own power and had not yet totally surrendered it to the Lord.

One of the final pretrip ceremonies took place after our Heaven on Wheels (CMA Chapter 48) Chapter Meeting in June, just eighteen days before the start of the trip. One of the ways CMA ministers to bikers is by doing bike blessings. My new Road King that would be my ride for the trip had not been "blessed" yet. I asked my good friend and our chapter president, Mike McClain, if he would do the honor of blessing my bike. Mike is a great man of God and tremendous servant/leader in our chapter. Having him bless my bike provided the finishing touch to my preparations. Thank you, Mike McClain, and all the members of Heaven on Wheels for your friendship over the years and especially for the prayer and support you poured over Jan and me throughout this adventure.

The day of departure finally arrived. The plan was for Jan and me to leave from our office in Topeka at 11:00 a.m. in Friday, June 24, and ride down to Idabel, Oklahoma, the official starting line for the official ride.

I was in the office Friday morning, but I wasn't working at all. I couldn't wait for eleven o'clock to get here, but at the same time, I felt there were things I needed to get done before I left and I was just running out of time.

About ten o'clock, Skip and Brenda arrived at the office. They had taken off work that day in order to come pray with us before we left. Rod "Tarzan" Falley also came by for the same reason. These people showing up meant more to me than I can ever tell them. I was so wound up by the time they got there; I'm sure they wondered whether I appreciated their appearance or not. I love you guys and will never forget the support you provided throughout the entire adventure.

I also never realized how worried for me everyone, including Jan, was. This send-off prayer time began to feel more like a funeral service than a send-off. I was never worried for my own safety and was quite surprised and even a little miffed at times when people expressed just how concerned they were.

Finally, at ten forty-five, we went outside to finally load the bikes. We circled up right there in the parking lot, and we prayed over the entire trip one last time. At eleven o'clock sharp, it was kickstands up, and Jan and I were finally on our way.

It was a 425-mile ride to get to Idabel, Oklahoma, the official starting point for the ride. We checked into the Super 8 as recommended on the Iron Butt website. About eighty thirty, after we got settled into our room, we walked down the road to a nice little Mexican restaurant for dinner. There was a ton of both excitement and nervousness as we talked about "the ride." It was almost surreal that it was actually about to happen.

Back in the room, I was trying to get a good night's sleep so I could at least begin day 1 fully rested. I finally did get a little sleep, but I was far too excited to be able to do much more than catnap.

I was wide awake at four o'clock that Saturday morning. I loaded the bike, and by four thirty, we went ahead and rode over to the Shell station, the official starting line for the ride.

Not only was it the official starting line for the ride; it was also my official "stop" in Oklahoma.

We pulled up to one of pumps, and I got my first official receipt for the ride. It was time-stamped 4:45 a.m., June 25, 2016.

If all I had been doing was following the Iron Butt rules, I would have been ready to head on down the road, but I had also committed to meet someone at every official stop and let them know that Jesus loves them.

As you might imagine, there were not many people around the Shell station in Idabel, Oklahoma, at four forty-five on a Saturday morning. The only person on the premises was the clerk inside the store. I put the first Bible of the trip in my back pocket, and Jan and I walked into the store.

I introduced myself to the young man behind the counter and told him the story of what I was about to do. I also told him that I wanted him to know that Jesus loved him. He was all smiles and, as he put it, "blown away" that I was talking to him. I asked him if we could pray with him. He came right out from behind the counter, and Jan and I prayed for him right there in the middle of the store.

What an awesome way to begin the ride. I had just made a new friend that seemed to really need to hear that Jesus loved him. And the fact that my wife got to experience that with me made it all that much more special.

Back to the bikes. One final check. A huge embrace between Jan and me, and at five o'clock on the dot, I headed south for New Boston, Texas, and Jan headed north for home. The ride was officially underway.

CHAPTER 3
GOD'S POSITIONING SYSTEM (MY GPS)

Before I start getting into the specifics of the journey, I want to spend a little time on one of the most important lessons I learned during the months leading up to the trip and the nearly twelve thousand miles of the actual trip. I know that probably seems strange, but to fully understand and appreciate just how profound this lesson was, I need to share a little bit of background first.

I'm sure everyone know what a GPS is. It seems most people don't go anywhere these days without their GPS. However, I'm an old Boy Scout and very proud of my navigational skills. I have always had a keen sense of direction. I have always been able to visualize my route on the map. I study my map and the route before I set out on a trip. By the time I actually travel, I've got the entire route memorized and seldom have to refer to the map again once the trip is underway.

Over the years, whenever Jan would suggest that we get a GPS, I would question, "Why? You've got *me*! I'm your personal GPS, babe!" Once they started putting GPS on smartphones, we actually tried it a couple of times. I guarantee you that I could plan a much better route using my atlas than what that silly GPS gave us. Not only did I not like the route it chose, but the way it gave the voice commands was totally confusing to me. The result of trying to use the GPS was getting totally lost, nearly destroying my phone, and being extremely grateful that I had also brought my atlas along—just in case.

When I first started planning the 48 States Plus Alaska ride, I found several routes online. One of the routes I discovered online started from Idabel, Oklahoma. I studied that route for hours, looking at it from satellite level down to street level. There were ten required checkpoints, which obviously had to be included in the route. I used an online route planner to tweak the suggested route to fit my liking. It took me several weeks to get my route dialed in to my liking, but I eventually had what I thought was the perfect route.

Once I had the route laid out, I spent hours and hours visualizing the ride. I was memorizing every detail of the entire 8,800-mile route. I identified the town I would stop in for every state in order to get my receipt for that state. I memorized the highway numbers and bypass options for the major metropolitan areas. I knew the first four days would be the most challenging as I would be in more than thirty states in those initial grueling days of the ride. Not only would I be touching a bunch of states, but I would be navigating through and around some of the large metropolises in the United States. On day 1 it was Atlanta, Georgia. Day 2 would take me through Washington, DC and the outskirts of Philadelphia, Pennsylvania, before I would shut down for the night on Staten Island, New York, in the home of my son Aaron and his family. Day 3 would begin in New York City and include Boston by noon. Day 4 would be Cleveland, Chicago, and Minneapolis.

As I approached the final weeks of preparation, I was confident. I had already visualized literally the entire trip over and over and knew every highway and intersection by heart. On the Saturday of Memorial Day weekend, a mere four weeks before the official start of the ride, I did one final dress rehearsal. I loaded my motorcycle with all the bags, sleeping bag, tent, and air mattress exactly as I intended to carry everything for the ride. The plan was to ride to Dallas, Texas, to have lunch with my son JR and his wife, Amanda, and ride home.

JR picked a BBQ joint in the north part of Dallas. When I stopped for gas about an hour north of Dallas, I decided to put the address for the restaurant into my GPS and just see how it worked. I don't know Dallas, and I really hadn't studied the map enough to feel confident in getting to this particular restaurant, which was a couple of miles off of the freeway. With the GPS linked to the Bluetooth in my helmet, I thought maybe it would get me where I needed to go.

Much to my amazement, the new GPS worked exceedingly well. It walked me right to my destination without the least bit of confusion. It was also the exact route I would have chosen if I had mapped it myself. All of a sudden, I had a new tool at my disposal to help me, especially as I worked my way through and around all of the *huge* cities east of the Mississippi River. I was really excited about the prospects, even if I was still somewhat skeptical about the GPS for the long haul.

When I was in the motel in Idabel, Oklahoma, the night before the start of the ride, I plugged Jackson, Mississippi, into the GPS. The route it gave me was exactly the same route that I had mapped with my online planner. Wow. This is working pretty well! I decided to use the GPS from the get-go. Ten miles before a route change, the GPS would alert me. Two miles before a route change, the GPS would alert me. This was *great*. Now I didn't have to worry about remembering every single route change. I was getting reminders right in my ear. All I had to do was listen and respond appropriately.

It was about two o'clock in the first afternoon. I was south of Jackson, Mississippi, on my way to Mobile, Alabama, when all of a sudden I heard the GPS saying something about saving time if I took a different route. This command caught me totally by surprise, as it was the first time I had heard that sort of command. I have already explained my extreme lack of confidence in my GPS being able to find the best route. And I had just spent nearly a year and a half planning this trip, and no stupid machine was going to "reroute" me on a whim.

I ignored this initial "reroute" from the GPS. Within five miles of passing the junction where the GPS was telling me to reroute, I found myself at a complete standstill for no apparent reason. I came over a hill, and all I could see for as far as I could see was a line of vehicles, all basically at a complete standstill. It took me over three hours to make it to Mobile, so I was now over two hours behind schedule. Man, was I kicking myself for not listening to my GPS.

On day 2, it got me to DC and beyond without incident. On day 3, it rerouted me around Boston due to unexpected delays on the planned route. On day 4, I took a wrong turn at Cleveland and suddenly found myself headed for Toledo, because I was sure the GPS was wrong and I knew better. I was rerouted at least three or four times in Chicago as the GPS maneuvered me around midday traffic situations. I was learning to listen to my GPS and at the same time learning to submit to its commands instead of relying on my own abilities. I also learned that I could not talk on the phone and hear commands from the GPS. More than once, when I was talking to Jan on the phone, I would hear a beep in my ear, indicating the GPS was trying to alert me of a route change or a reroute. I had to abruptly end the phone conversation in order to free up the Bluetooth for the GPS. I hung up on my son and hung up on several of my friends. I even hung up on my mom so I could listen to my GPS.

God began to speak to my heart through the experience of hanging up on everyone that was supporting me through this journey in order to listen to my GPS. How often in life do I get caught up in listening to family and friends? How often in life do I get advice from people that really care about me and believe they are genuinely trying to help me? I'm not saying that I shouldn't listen to those people. I'm not even saying that I shouldn't, from time to time, seek out their advice. But most important of all, I need to be listening to my GPS—"God's Positioning System."

John 16:12–14 says, "I still have many things to say to you, but you cannot bear them now. When the Spirit of truth comes, he will guide you into all the truth, for he will not speak on his own authority, but whatever he hears he will speak, and he will declare to you the things that are to come. He will glorify me, for he will take what is mine and declare it to you."

Gaining wisdom from the Spirit is talked about in 1 Corinthians 2:6–10: "Yet among the mature we do impart wisdom, although it is not a wisdom of this age or of the rulers of this age, who are doomed to pass away. But we impart a secret and hidden wisdom of God, which God decreed before the ages for our glory. None of the rulers of this age understood this, for if they had, they would not have crucified the Lord of glory. But, as it is written, "What no eye has seen, nor ear heard, nor the heart of man imagined, what God has prepared for those who love him"—these things God has revealed to us through the Spirit. For the Spirit searches everything, even the depths of God."

Just like learning to recognize the voice of my GPS and trust the commands it was giving me was a challenge for me in the beginning, learning to recognize the voice of the Holy Spirit and submit to its leading is a challenge for most Christians. So just how do we accomplish this? First of all, we need to study our roadmap. Just as I spent hours and hours studying my atlas, God impressed on me that I need to be just as diligent in my daily walk to continually study my roadmap for life. The inspired and infallible Word of our Father, which has survived for thousands of years, contains every route number and every route change we will ever encounter on our journey through this life here on earth. It is absolutely imperative that we study our roadmap.

It is also essential to commit to prayer. Prayer is the channel the Lord has provided us to communicate with Him. We must pray, which includes time for listening and waiting to hear from the Lord. One of my first pastors, Pastor Curtis Fulton, who went home to be with the Lord just a few months before I made this trip, used to tell me, "You need to pray like it all depends on God. Then you need to work like it all depends on you." Pastor Fulton told me that when I was about twenty-five years old, and I've never forgotten it. It's been an excellent guide for my life. Thank you, Curtis.

Most new Christians struggle to distinguish what is truly the voice of the Holy Spirit. Just like the first time my GPS talked to me when I was not expecting it, I wasn't sure if it was the GPS or some other voice, maybe from the telephone. In time, I clearly recognized the GPS, even when it cut in unexpectedly to "reroute" me and help me avoid unnecessary delays and snarls. The more we communicate and the more we listen, the more familiar it all becomes.

While studying our roadmap and listening for His voice are two very important steps, we gain nothing until we finally surrender our will to that of the Spirit. When I began my journey, I was convinced that I knew the best route. I was using the GPS, in the beginning, as just a good safety net, a good backup plan in case I couldn't remember which route to take somewhere along the way. I was looking at the GPS as something that I would call upon in a pinch, but I certainly didn't need it for every mile or every turn along the way. I got this. I can handle this. But I've got the GPS just in case.

It wasn't until I took the wrong turn in Cleveland, Ohio, and found myself headed to Toledo that I finally decided to completely surrender to the GPS. I had to admit that I didn't have it, that I couldn't handle it on my own, that I needed the GPS to lead the way. We have to surrender in the same way to the leading of the Holy Spirit. We tend to think we got it, that we can handle it. To achieve the very best that God has for us, we must learn to walk perfectly in His will and follow the roadmap He has for us.

Finally, God showed me just how important it is to shut out the world so we can truly hear His voice. We are bombarded by noise on TV, radio, the internet, and a myriad of other media. Frequently, it doesn't even seem like noise, because it might be a trusted source, maybe even an individual that loves us and has our best interest in mind. But just like on the road when I had to hang up on my wife, my friends, and even my mom in order to listen to the GPS, sometimes, we're just going to have to "hang up" on the noise of the world and listen for the voice of the Holy Spirit.

The first time I had to do this with my wife, she was *very* upset. But once I was beyond the critical moments of instructions and rerouting, I was able to call her back and explain what had happened. Once she understood, she was actual thankful that I had hung up on her so I could stay on course. When you start surrendering to the leading of the Holy Spirit and blocking out the world in order to listen intently to your instructions from the Holy Spirit, your friends and family may not understand at first. That's okay. Hold fast to your commitment to follow God's Positioning System and let your circle know you still love them. Your life will be your testimony, and eventually they will understand as well.

CHAPTER 4
DIVINE APPOINTMENTS

I talked briefly about the prayer in the middle of the convenience store in Idabel. I want to spend just a little more time on that very first encounter now as we begin to get acquainted with a few of the individuals that God put in my path along the way. As I mentioned earlier, I had begun to feel an incredible burden for the people I was going to meet. Of course, I had no idea who they were. I just knew that the rules of the ride required me to stop in every state in order to get a receipt. God had laid it on my heart to take advantage of those stops to meet someone and let that person know that God loves them.

How would I know just who it was that God wanted me to talk to? How would these people react to a stranger walking up to them? I was nervous as all get out. While my friends were afraid for me and my safety, I was *only* worried about this assignment to find a total stranger, in a city where I have probably never been before, that isn't going to be upset by some weird guy on a motorcycle interrupting their busy schedule. To be completely honest with you, I wasn't just nervous or worried; I was completely petrified.

So when we arrived at the gas station that Saturday morning and there was only one person on the premises besides Jan and myself, it completely eliminated the question of "who" I was to talk to. Thank you, Jesus! Once I had finished gassing the bike and went inside talk to the young man, it was clear that I wasn't interrupting him. He was actually glad and excited that he had someone to talk to. And the reaction from him when I asked his permission to pray with him completely rested my anxiety. It was like the Lord was right by my side telling me, "Just relax and do your thing. *I got this.*" Again, thank you, Jesus!

Jan and I both embraced our new friend and walked out to the bikes with tears in our eyes. The motorcycle had not moved an inch yet, but the trip was definitely off and running with a huge bang of confirmation that the Lord was with me and He was going to use me and this trip in a mighty way. I gave Jan one last bear hug and giant kiss and headed south toward Texas with tears in my eyes and a song in my heart.

It was only about a half hour later when I arrived in New Boston, Texas. The only reason I needed to stop was to buy something in order to get my receipt and certify that I was actually in the state of Texas. I had a full tank of gas. As I approached New Boston, I realized that I could stop anywhere. I could stop at a doughnut shop (my favorite). I could stop at a pancake or waffle house (also my favorite). I could stop at a coffee shop or convenience store. Where did the Lord want me to stop? Where was the person that He wanted me to meet in Texas?

The confidence that I felt just a few miles back was waning quickly. I was completely intimidated by the task of discovering the person God wanted me to talk to. I got off the main highway in order to drive through town instead of bypassing it. I saw a doughnut shop, but to my surprise, I went right on by. Before I knew it, I was approaching the main highway again on the opposite end of New Boston. There was a convenience store with gas station on both sides of the street. I chose to pull into the one on my right instead of trying to cross traffic (even though, at 5:30 a.m. on a Saturday morning, traffic was *really* not an issue). I pulled up in front of the store, shut off the motorcycle, reached in my left-side saddlebag for my next Bible, and began to survey the situation. I spotted a young man putting gas in his car at the center island. He was wearing some sort of uniform, and I just had a sense that this young man was my divine appointment for Texas. I approached him, but since his back was toward me, I stayed back a bit until he finished fueling his vehicle.

I introduced myself to him, pointed to my motorcycle, and gave him a brief overview of what my mission was. I also noticed that his uniform was that of a correction officer. He told me that he was on his way home from work. I shared with him that I was very involved in prison ministry back in Kansas and that I have the utmost respect for everyone that serves as he does. I told him that I knew it was no accident that he and I were at this place at the same time because I wanted to let him know that Jesus loved him. He said that he had grown up in a Christian home, but he had fallen away from church and knew he needed to get reconnected. I asked if I could pray for him. Without hesitation, he said yes. When I finished praying for him, he was crying. I was crying. I wished him all the best and headed for my motorcycle.

For an instant, I felt an urge to ask him if I could take a picture of us, but before I could even turn around to ask the question, the Lord stopped me. He impressed on me that this was not about collecting trophies. This was not about what I was doing. It was about what God was doing. I almost got back on my motorcycle and took off without getting a receipt. I stopped my leg midflight and marched into the store to figure out what I was going to buy so I could get my receipt. I wasn't thinking ahead when I was back in Idabel and had really stocked up on water. I didn't need gas. I had made the decision months back that I was not going to buy anything that I would have to carry with me. If I couldn't pour it in my gas tank or in my mouth, I wasn't going to buy it. No souvenirs.

At this first stop, my receipt was for chocolate milk. I chugged it down as fast as I could, got back on my bike, and headed east for Arkansas. My stop in Arkansas was scheduled to be at Texarkana. I saw city-limit signs for Texarkana, saw a McDonald's, and pulled in. As I was dismounting and reaching for my next Bible, I suddenly questioned where I was. An elderly couple was just getting out of their truck to head into the McDonald's, so I approached them. "Am I in Texas or Arkansas?" I asked them. "Arkansas is just down the road," the gentleman told me. By now he was curious, so I went through my spiel. He warned me that once I got headed south and got past Texarkana, there weren't any more stops before I got into Louisiana.

After a few minutes, I was able to get on with my journey. Almost immediately upon exiting the McDonald's parking lot, I was into the interchange and moving onto Highway 71 headed south to Shreveport, Louisiana. I was bypassing Texarkana. It was only three or four miles until I was approaching the interchange to leave Texarkana. I decided to go on through the interchange to look for my stop in Arkansas. Less than a half mile past the interchange, I found a little run-down convenience store and gas station. It was still only about 6:30 a.m. Most everyone at this store seemed to be stocking up for a day at the lake. They were very preoccupied with their own mission for the day. I went inside to see if things were any different inside. I bought another carton of chocolate milk and went back outside with my Bible still in my pocket. As I sat there trying to figure out what I was going to do, I noticed a very "rumpled" man putting gas in a very rusty vehicle that I wasn't sure would even run. I knew why I had gone past my exit.

I approached the man and began the conversation by asking him if he was from around these parts. He said that he and his wife had just moved here from Indiana. About this time, his wife came out of the store (she must have been in the restroom when I went inside because I had not seen her). She was even more "rumpled" than her husband was. He explained to me that his wife's mother has passed away recently in Indiana. It had been extremely hard on his wife. Her aunt had pleaded with them to move to Texarkana because they would be able to find work there and get their lives back on track. He went on to say that things had not worked out at all like the aunt had told them. They felt like they were about at the end of their rope.

After listening to him tell their story, I told him a little bit of what I doing and asked him if I could pray for him and wife. He motioned to the passenger seat of the car where his wife was sitting and said I'd have to ask her. We walked around the car to speak with his wife. I don't know if the window didn't work or if she just didn't want to roll it down, but she opened the door just a tiny crack. I leaned down close to speak through the crack and asked her if I could pray for her and her husband real quick. Her response was a very terse, "Make it quick 'cause I got to go get my meds." I took the liberty to open the door just enough to slip my right hand inside the car and lay it on the lady's shoulder. I grabbed her husband's arm with my left hand and prayed the quickest and most fervent prayer I have ever prayed in my life. I let them know that Jesus loved them very much and that I was going to continue to pray for them.

Despite my order to "make it quick," once I finished praying, she pushed the door open and proceeded to pour her heart out to me for several minutes. I gave them both a hug and headed toward Shreveport. I was barely two hours into my journey, and God had already allowed me to participate in three totally awesome prayers and connect with four people that were total strangers to me, but very precious to Jesus. He was confirming *big-time* that He was leading the way. I was in tears for the third time already as I pulled back onto the highway. I was wondering how much more of this I could take!

Something that I never expected at all was the emotion I was feeling as I left the couple in Texarkana. I wasn't carrying much cash with me. Listening to this couple talk about their struggles, I was compelled to offer them some money. I was in a real predicament. I was totally frustrated, wanting to help in some more tangible way than simply pray for them. But I didn't have any money to offer them. I'm sure this emotional tug-of-war also contributed to my wonderment of how much more of this could I take. I struggled with how I handled that situation for the better part of the first two days of the trip. By the end of the second day, I had already been in seventeen states. I continued to have incredible appointments and was privileged to meet fourteen more amazing people just in the first two days, but none of them lingered in my thoughts the way the couple from Texarkana did. I was haunted by a sense of failure.

On Sunday afternoon, day 2 of the trip, on a long boring stretch of I-81 headed across Virginia toward Washington, DC, the Lord finally spoke to me very clearly and reminded me that He had asked me to "tell them that I love them." I had done that. He didn't ask me to build the entire wall. My job was to lay one of the stones. There are others that can lay more stones. Sometimes I might be putting down one of the very first stones. Somewhere along the way, I might get the opportunity to place the very last stone so I could see the completed work. It was not for me to worry about the timing. That was God's. A peace came over me, and I no longer felt like a failure, but I have continued to think about and pray for this couple more than anybody I met in the forty-nine states. Even though I included my phone number and email address on the letter in every one of the Bibles, and I even pointed it out to this couple, I have never heard from them since that fateful Saturday morning. I often wonder about them and would like to hear that they have found peace in their new life in Arkansas. I would encourage you to add them to your prayer list and lift them up along with me. I'm not sharing names in this essay, but I'm sure when you lift up the couple from Texarkana, Arkansas, that God will know exactly who you're talking about.

CHAPTER 5
ADVENTURES WITHIN THE ADVENTURE

As you can see, God's handprints were all over this trip from the moment I turned it over to Him. And while I am *still* in awe of everything that He allowed me to witness along the way, I did not spend the entire time testifying on His behalf. There were a few incidents along the way that definitely contributed to the adventure of the trip. Some were funny as they unfolded, and some are funny now as I look back on them. There were a few times when I felt incredibly challenged for a variety of different reasons, and I praise the Lord that He carried me through each of those situations unscathed.

On the very first night, I experienced the first "ah-oh" moment. This was the very end of a very long first day. Throughout the entire planning process, my intention was to sleep in rest areas as much as possible. I was praying that there would be an obvious opportunity for me to bed down when I reached my one thousand miles each day. It was approaching 11:00 PM, and I'd been up since 4:00 AM after getting very little sleep the night before. I had just crossed from Georgia into South Carolina and, by my odometer, just passed the one-thousand mark when I saw a sign announcing a rest area just ahead. Perfect timing! Yeah, God!

This was a beautiful rest area. I promise you, we have nothing even close to this in Kansas, mainly because we don't have the incredibly tall pine trees that covered this area. A nice, clean restroom on one side of the drive and several picnic tables on the other side of the drive under the umbrella of the pines. As I got off my motorcycle, I noticed a sign: "No Camping." I had my tent, my sleeping bag, and my air mattress rolled up on the seat behind me for this very purpose, and I had found the perfect spot. How could this be? I was tired. I was in a place I'd never been before and had no idea when I would find the next "perfect spot." Jan had been griping at me for more than an hour to get shut down and get some rest. Quite frankly, I didn't feel like going any further right then. I stood right in front of the sign just staring at it and trying to figure out what I was going to do.

It came down to the definition of "camping." I concluded that I was not "camping." I was just going to "rest" for a few hours. Since this was a "rest area," there should be no problem with me using it for such purpose. So instead of setting up the tent, I simply rolled out my air mattress on top of the picnic table closest to where I parked, crawled up on top of the table, and started resting. Even though I was incredibly tired, I was having a difficult time falling asleep. I lay on top of that table just staring up through the pine trees and responding to the messages that were coming in from my family and friends that had been tracking me all day and could see that I was finally stationary. Even though I was all by myself in a place that I had never been in my life, I felt surrounded by love and support. I was staring up at an amazing scene that I would never ever see in Kansas.

It was close to midnight before I finally dozed off, and I woke up at 2:45 AM. I was wide awake immediately and felt as if I had just slept eight hours, so I decided to get started on day 2. Best of all, nobody bothered me at all about "resting" on top of the table. And no one messed with my motorcycle. So far, so good. Thank you, Jesus!

The next moment that I want to share was not funny at all as it was unfolding. It became a huge lesson in why it is so important to study a map and have a big-picture view of your route in addition to following the GPS. Back in the chapter about the GPS, I mentioned Pastor Fulton's saying, "You have to pray like it all depends on God, and then you have to work like it all depends on you." God gave us a brain for a purpose. He expects us to use it. But He also expects us to listen to Him.

On day 3, I was getting broke to following the GPS and beginning to recognize when it would cut in unexpectedly to reroute me due to unexpected traffic delays on the planned route. My plan was to simply follow I-95 all the way through Boston right up to Kittery, Maine. I was barely into Massachusetts when I suddenly heard the command to reroute onto I-495 to save time. I knew this was a bypass that would bring me back onto I-95 north of Boston. I decided I was going to wait until I got back onto I-95 to make my stop in Massachusetts.

It took me about an hour and a half to make it back to I-95. I immediately began looking for an exit for my Massachusetts certification stop, but I also realized that the mile markers had reset to 3 then 4 then 5. I was approaching a tollbooth, and as I got close enough to read the signs, they were talking about New Hampshire. When I asked the tollbooth attendant if I was really in New Hampshire, she gave me an extremely puzzled and somewhat amused nod of her head. I had just spent about two hours in the state of Massachusetts and did not have any way to prove it. For a moment, I was tempted to just go on, but I didn't want to let this little miscalculation destroy my opportunity to certify the entire ride.

I decided that I would turn around at my first opportunity, get back down to Massachusetts, and get my receipt. I had to go another ten miles into New Hampshire before I came to an exit where I could get turned around and headed back south. About thirty minutes after I went through the tollboth going north, I was going back through the tollbooth in the opposite direction. Literally right over the border back in Massachusetts, there was a visitor center with a little souvenir shop. I bought the only souvenir of the entire ride, a book with a short biography of all the signers of the Declaration of Independence, and I had my receipt certifying that I had indeed been in Massachusetts.

Because of I-495 and I-95 coming together right there, I was able to see that there indeed was no exit to this visitor center from the route I was on when I came by the first time. That made me feel a little better. It also meant that I had to do a whole bunch of weaving and turning in order to get back on I-95 north again. Just as soon as I made my way back onto the freeway, I was back in New Hampshire. Guess what. About an hour after I went through the tollbooth the first time, I was pulling back up to the same tollbooth and the same puzzled look from the young lady attendant. I just handed her my money and proceeded on my way to Kittery.

As I approached the exit where I had turned around, I was getting commands from the GPS that my exit to Kittery, Maine, was just ahead. When I turned around and went back to Massachusetts, I was only two miles from my checkpoint in Kittery. I wasn't looking at a map. I was simply listening to the GPS. I didn't realize how close I was to Kittery when I turned around and went back. Boy, am I frustrated now. Oh well. It is about 12:30 p.m. on day 3, and I just arrived in Maine, the farthest northeast point of the route. *Wow!*

So now I needed to figure out how to get across New Hampshire and Vermont and end up on I-90 in upstate New York. The GPS gave me my route, which meant I was to head back south on I-95. To get back to I-95, the GPS was taking me straight south over a bridge instead of going back west over the bridge I came in on. When I got over the bridge, the interchange was exactly the same one where I had turned around about an hour earlier to head back to Massachusetts. I could only laugh at the situation. I was now headed back south on I-95 for the second time in a little more than an hour.

As I was approaching the area of the tollbooth for the fourth time, I was routed onto sort of a frontage road that took me around the tollbooth, so I was able to avoid paying a fourth toll. Thank you, Jesus! By the time I was exiting onto my route headed west, I could literally see the visitor center in Massachusetts. Again, I could only laugh at the situation. But what an incredible lesson about the importance of both praying and listening to the Lord but also doing our part to be able to see the entire picture and understand the path that He has set us on.

Day 7 was probably the most boring days of the trip, and it was also one of the most eventful days of the trip. I know that sounds contradictory, but it's the absolute truth. I started the morning in Needles, California, the most southwest point of the trip. I had arrived the night before in an incredible thunderstorm. You can't prove it by me that it never rains in Southern California. I thought the weather was clearing out overnight and had even packed my rain gear back in the case. When I was loading the bike to head out, I could see lightning to the north, so I pulled the rain gear back out and put it on. Good thing I did.

I got back into the storm just as I headed north toward Las Vegas. I got hit with a couple of wind gusts that felt like they were going to blow me right off the highway. The rain was coming down in sheets. It was still dark. The wind was blowing me all over the place. I can honestly say this was the only time on the entire trip that I considered turning around and going back. I was very uncomfortable. I pulled over on the shoulder to collect my thoughts, and as I sat there, a couple of other vehicles passed me headed in the same direction I was going. I figured if they could continue, I could as well.

It was still raining fiercely when I pulled back onto the highway. I was focused on the stripes of the highway and could only see a very short way in front of me. All of a sudden, the stripes simply disappeared, and water was spraying out from my tires. I don't know for sure how deep this first washout was, but I'm pretty sure it came up to the lower part of my motor. The water was coming up my legs into my lap and coming over the top of my windshield. Of course, the water wasn't as deep as my windshield, but it did come up over the top of it. Thankfully, this washout was only about fifteen or twenty yards wide, and I was able to keep the motor from flooding out. I hit four or five similar washouts over about a ten-minute span and obviously made it through every one of them. I don't know if the first one was the worst or if it just felt that way because it caught me totally by surprise.

Just as it was starting to get a little bit light, I rounded a slight bend to see traffic at a complete stop. There was another washout except this one was about a quarter mile wide and looked like a raging river. Traffic from both directions was stopped. There was another motorcycle up ahead, so I pulled up beside him. He had been sitting there for three hours. We sat there together for about an hour. We could see the water gradually slowing down and the span getting a little narrower. Finally, a Chevy Impala from the other side of the washout decided to give it a go. Right in the middle, the water was still deep enough to come up to the side of the car. Not very much, but enough that I'm certain the driver was really second-guessing his decision to make a run at it. All of a sudden, the water was pushing the car sideways, and we all thought he was going downriver. Fortunately, he was able to gun it, get just enough traction to get past the deepest part of the flow before he was washed off the road.

He made it, but everyone that was watching knew we needed to wait just a little longer before we attempted the same thing. In just a few minutes, a semitruck from our side made the crossing, and then a semi came across from the other side without any incident. The water was starting to go down fairly quickly now. All the four wheel vehicles were getting on their way. The two motorcycles waited until everyone else had gone, and then we finally waded in as well. By now, the washout was down to a hundred yards or so, and only for a few yards in the very middle did water get up to our feet. We just kept moving, kept the engines revved, and actually made it fairly easily. I really believe our timing was about perfect. If we had gone much sooner, the water would have been deep enough and flowing fast enough that it would have probably pushed our bikes right on downstream. Thank you, Jesus! I made it to Las Vegas about 8:00 a.m. when I had expected to be there by no later than six thirty. I was definitely way behind schedule, but at least I was headed in the right direction.

The entire rest of that day was spent on I-15 making my way from Las Vegas up to Salt Lake City. This is absolutely a beautiful country, but it was also day 7; I was very tired, and there was no reason to stop except for gas. Also, on the day that I was expecting to be dealing with incredible heat, I was actually wearing my fleece pullover and rain gear most of the day. What a weird day!

At Salt Lake City, I picked up I-80 and headed east for about an hour so I could touch Wyoming. Then it was back west to I-15 again and headed north. It was about 10:00 p.m. when I came up on a rest area. I was hoping to make it a little farther north and closer to Butte, Montana, before I shut down for the night, but I was again seeing lightning up ahead, so I decided to pull into this rest area. There was a perfect little grassy area just to side of the main building, and it was the softest, greenest grass you could ever imagine. I knew this was the exact spot for me to pitch my tent and ride out whatever weather those clouds were bringing my way. No sooner had I gotten the tent set up and my stuff inside than the rain began. The wind blew a little bit, but nothing like what I was in earlier that morning. The rain lasted only a half hour or so. The tent was doing great. Between my air mattress and that incredibly soft grass, I had the most comfortable sleeping arrangement I had had in more than a week.

The rain had stopped, and I had apparently fallen asleep when, all of a sudden, it sounded like my air mattress had sprung a major leak. It woke me up with a start, but the noise just kept going and kept going. I knew there just wasn't that much air in my mattress. What the heck is going on? As I was feeling around for the source of this commotion, I bumped my head on something hard under the floor of the tent. When I put my hand on it, I felt something swirl under my fingers. That freaked me out big-time. Then I realized what was happening. I had pitched my tent right on top of one of the sprinkler heads for the automatic irrigation system.

For the next fifteen minutes, I lay there praying that my tent floor was tough enough to withstand the pressure of the water. I didn't want to think about what would happen if that sprinkler head came through the floor of my tent and soaked me and all my stuff. Well, the floor made it. Nobody and nothing got wet except the underneath side of my tent floor. In just a few minutes after everything shut off, I was back asleep and finally completed with a very long day of boredom sandwiched between two spine-tingling events on either end. As I stated at the beginning of this chapter, I am inspired to this day as I think back on not only these events but several other similar events where God protected me, guided me, and allowed me to experience the wonder and beauty of His work in a very up-close and personal way, for which I am eternally grateful. Thank you, Jesus!

While day 7 was provided the most extreme emotional swing of the trip, day 8 provided the most extreme temperature swing of the trip. When I started from my little campsite on top of the sprinkler head in southern Montana, the temperature was in the low forties. I have ridden in very cold temperatures in Kansas, even down into the twenties, but that has been in the winter when you're expecting it, your blood is much thicker, and you're definitely dressed for it. I had only brought water-resistant gloves to protect my hands from the rain. Neither had I brought my insulated boots that I would have been wearing in forty-degree weather in Kansas.

By the time I stopped for my receipt in Butte, Montana, I was flat out *cold*. I went into the convenience store and bought a cup of hot chocolate and just sat in the warmth of the store for several minutes. Even though I knew I was just a few hours from completing the 48 States portion of my ride, at this moment, sitting there thinking about how cold I was, I *really* wasn't looking forward to getting back on my motorcycle. I spent about thirty minutes trying to warm up, but still I felt chilled when I forced myself back onto the route. It wasn't until I got to Spokane, Washington, that I finally didn't feel cold anymore. Notice I said I didn't feel cold anymore. I didn't feel warm; I just didn't feel cold anymore. Thank you, Jesus!

At Spokane, I had to head south in order to touch the last of the 48 States. It took me an hour and a half or so to get to Umatilla, Oregon. By the time I got to Umatilla, the temperature was in the eighties, which is really quite warm in that part of the country. I stood under the canopy of the gas station where I got my receipt for the forty-eighth and final state and was able to take off *all* my coats and gloves and just soak up the warmth you expect to feel on July 2 in the northern hemisphere. Thank you, Jesus!

I headed back north toward Canada and Alaska. I crossed into Canada from Oroville, Washington, at about 5:00 PM. As I passed a sign in Oroville that read "Canada – 3 Miles," I also saw a time and temperature sign that said, "97." *Wow!* I promise you, I was not cold anymore. In the four hours I had spent crossing Washington State from south to north, I had drunk almost every ounce of water I was carrying in my camel pack. When I stopped for gas in Omak, Washington, the locals there were freaking out about how ridiculously *hot* it was, even for July 2. I just thought back a few hours to how cold I had been and smiled. I had just experienced a temperature swing of nearly sixty degrees in a day. Don't get that in Kansas very often.

I spent the last night of the journey in Kamloops, British Columbia. According to my GPS, I was only 750 miles from my final destination. I left the Days Inn at my usual 5:00 AM and was now back in all my warmest clothes as the temperature was back in the upper forties to begin the ninth and final day of my trip. I was less than thirty minutes into the ride when it began to rain lightly. I stopped at my first opportunity to get off the highway and donned my rain gear once again.

I traveled in light to moderate rain from before the sun came up almost continually until about 4:00 PM that afternoon. I was really getting sick and tired of being cold and wet. I had spent way more time preparing for extreme heat than I had spent preparing for cold. About three thirty that afternoon, I rolled into Houston, British Columbia. I was thinking, *Houston! It's* got *to be warm in Houston! Right?* The sign on the bank said eight degrees. I realize that is eight degrees Celsius, but when you're sick and tired of being cold and wet, seeing 8 on the temperature sign doesn't do much to warm your bones. Not long after heading on up the road from Houston, it finally quit raining, but I never saw the sun that day and the final forty miles into Hyder, Alaska, was in fog, which felt very cold and wet. Once I got in my room shortly after 7:00 PM, I was able to enjoy the longest, warmest shower I have ever experienced in my life. Thank you, Jesus.

CHAPTER 6

THE BLESSINGS JUST
KEEP ON COMING

I talked about the divine appointments that God led me to as I began the trip and what incredible blessing each of these encounters brought me. If that were the end of the blessings, the entire trip would have been worth it. When I was a young person, there was a radio disc jockey named Casey Kasem, whose signature phrase was "And the hits just keep on rolling." As I continued my journey, day after day, "the blessings just kept on coming." Before I finish, I have to share a few more of the stories of these blessings with you.

I'm not going to talk about every single person I met, and just as before, I'm not going to use names, but I believe you will understand why the encounters I have chosen to share with you meant so much to me. Hopefully, as you read, your heart will be as moved as mine was and you can join me in praying for these individuals.

In Jackson, Mississippi, I met a young father who was driving a van full of very enthusiastic and energetic teenage girls. The driver was the father of one of the girls, and he was driving his daughter's cheerleading team to a competition and acting as an adult sponsor for the weekend event. That was impressive enough, seeing his calm demeanor in the midst of all this enthusiasm, but as he told me his story, I could not help but rejoice. This man was an over-the-road truck driver. He had been sent out on an expected run just forty-eight hours prior to the time that he was supposed to begin chauffeuring the cheerleaders. He had driven all day and all night in order to get home in time to be a dad. I would have been totally wiped out and as grouchy and an old bear, but not this dad. He only talked about how blessed he was to be able to be a part of his daughter's exciting experience. Yes, I prayed for him and for the cheerleaders, but I am the one who was blessed. As I topped off my tank on the Road King, the girls were piling back into the van and headed off to their competition. *Wow*, God. Thank you for blessing me once again.

The next morning I was in Ashville, North Carolina. It was 5:30 a.m. I was literally running on fumes and needed a gas station— *now*. Even though it was dark and I was in a town I had never visited in my life, I could just sense that it was not a very good place to be stopping for anything, but I really had no choice. When I pulled into the station, it was lit by lights from the canopies over the two pump islands. Under the canopy closest to the road was a *Dukes of Hazard*-looking car (only it was that nice), with the hood open and a kid underneath. The doors and windows to the store were covered with bars. I was really excited to be able to stop here.

I could see an attendant working inside, so when I finished getting my gas, I went inside to meet the attendant. He was a middle-aged gentleman that seemed relieved when he saw the Christian Motorcyclists Association patches on my vest. I shared my story with him and asked if there was anything I could pray about for him. He proceeded to share about his son, who was in the grips of drugs and alcohol. He had been raised in the church and knew how he should be living but was totally consumed by his addictions. The attendant and his wife have been praying for him for years and feeling defeated.

To fully appreciate the rest of this particular blessing, I have to share with you now the "randomness" of what happened next. You see, I started the trip with fifty CMA "Hope for the Highway" Bibles in my saddlebag. Before packing the Bibles, I had placed a copy of my letter and the Jesus Film app instructions in each one of the Bibles. There was no system to this project. I simply grabbed a signed and folded copy of the letter, stuck an instruction card for the Jesus Film app inside the folded letter, and then simply flipped open the next Bible and stuck it in. When I got to a stop, I reached into the saddlebag and grabbed the next Bible on the stack.

Now back to Ashville. As the attendant was sharing the story of his son, I began to think about one of the testimonies that is in the "Hope for the Highway." There are several testimonies sprinkled throughout this particular version of the Bible. The one that came to my mind is by John Ogden Jr. John was raised in a Christian home and had accepted Jesus at a young age, but by the time he was a young adult, his life was consumed by addictions and didn't look anything like the walk of a Christian. I pulled the Bible from my pocket to thumb through it in search of this testimony, and it fell open to the exact spot. The letter had been placed right on that testimony. "Random"? Right!

Later that day, I got to Washington, DC. It was really hot by then, and traffic was terrible. I pulled in for gas in College Park, Maryland, which is right on the outside of the beltway around DC. Another gas station in a not-so-good neighborhood. This was the only time I just didn't feel the spirit telling me who to talk to. On the outside island was a carload of extremely loud individuals that were cursing and threatening each other. It was difficult to imagine myself walking up to them and trying to inject myself into their "conversation."

The door to the convenience store was locked and barred. There was bulletproof glass surrounding the "store" where the attendant was stationed. To order, you looked into the "store," pointed or yelled, and placed your payment in the drawer that came out like the one at the drive-through at the bank. Once she rang up your payment, in my case for a diet Pepsi, here came my drink out in the drawer. I actually tried to talk to the lady attendant, but she looked like she might be high herself, or struggling to not be high. She actually looked away when I tried to talk to her.

Then, the third possibility in this setting was from the vehicle at island closest to the "store." I watched as a young man that was obviously paraplegic pulled a wheelchair from his car, lifted himself into the chair, and rolled to the pump. I was afraid my question, "Is there anything I can pray about for you?" would seem incredibly obvious and maybe even insulting, so I actually turned to put the Bible back in the saddlebag. Just as I was reaching for the lid, I heard a voice behind me. "Could you help me, please?" I turned back to see the young man in the chair. The insert for the card was at the very tip of his reach, and he just couldn't get it.

Now, almost in embarrassment, I went to his rescue, only to find that the problem was with the machine, not his limitations. I tried to reset the machine, but no success. Finally, we had to resort to asking the attendant for her help. She seemed totally petrified at the thought of leaving the security of her perch behind the bulletproof glass, but after a bit of pleading, she finally came out and got the pump's card reader working for us.

In all this hubbub, I got a chance to speak with this man. He was from California and, within the last thirty days, had moved to Washington, DC, to work for the Department of Labor. He was terrified about surviving in this whole new environment and culture. He was also totally grateful when I asked if I could pray with him and then gave him his Bible. *Wow!* I almost turned my back on this blessing. Thank you, God.

But He wasn't done yet. Instead of getting on the Road King, I looked through the bulletproof glass and noticed the attendant was watching what had been happening since she locked herself back in her haven. I lifted the lid on the saddlebag, grabbed another Bible, and walked back up to the window. This time, she didn't turn away. She actually leaned down to the drawer so she could hear me better. I prayed for her and placed the Bible in the drawer. She was already reading it when I finally did pull away.

On the morning of day 3 in Wyoming, Rhode Island, I encountered the only rejection of the entire trip. I had stopped for gas at a convenience store. As I was doing my usual thing of scanning the property for who I was going to approach, my eyes focused on a man about my age that was driving a van for what appeared to be a heating and cooling contractor. It looked like he might even be there to do some work instead of being a customer. At any rate, once I fueled,

I headed into the store. When the gentleman and I approached each other, I pulled the Bible out of my pocket, began to introduce myself to him, like I had already done in eighteen other states. My presentation was met with a raised hand, the stop sign, him shaking his head and telling me he was not at all interested in that stuff. He was not rude. He just made it very clear that he was not interested in talking to me about Jesus. The moment I was so afraid of before the trip began had just happened, but it wasn't terrible experience I had feared. I told him to have a great day and turned and headed back outside.

While I was inside, a young family had pulled up to the other side of the gas pump from where my motorcycle was parked. When I walked up to them, they began asking me questions about how far I was traveling. As I explained my trip, they were totally excited to have run into me and were thrilled that they were the proud recipients of the Bible for Rhode Island. Another reminder that God is always in control, that nothing ever surprises Him, and I needed to slow down, lean on Him more, and stop depending on my own abilities.

About eleven hours and six hundred winding and roller-coaster miles later on day 3, I stopped for gas on I-90 in upstate New York near Canastota. I had given my New York Bible to my daughter-in-law, Alison, when I stayed at their house at Staten Island, New York, the night before, so I was not planning to do anything on this stop in New York except get gas. As I was putting gas in my tank, I heard a voice from behind me say, "Hey, I really like your patch!" When I turned around, I saw a twentysomething young man, who was also riding a motorcycle, walking toward me. He was from Minnesota and was in the midst of road trip of his own. When he had left Minnesota, he felt like he was taking on a pretty aggressive trip that was taking him through eight or ten states and covering a couple of thousand miles over about a week. Quite frankly, that *is* an aggressive trip, and I let him know I was really proud to see such a young man already diving into this subculture that I love so much. He was also a Christian and wanted to hear about CMA. I pulled a Bible out of my saddlebag and showed him how to get on the CMA website to locate a chapter near his home in Minnesota.

When I pulled into that service area, in my mind, it was going to be a real quick stop. I was *way* behind schedule for the day because of all the backtracking earlier between Massachusetts and New Hampshire combined with the twisting and turning of getting across New Hampshire and Vermont. I didn't plan to give away a Bible on this stop. I was going to be in and out in five minutes and make up some time. Instead, I had one of the richest encounters of the entire journey. Again, God stepping in to teach me yet another lesson. He was reminding me not to limit Him. *My* plan was to give away *one* Bible in each state. Since I had left home with fifty Bibles, one for each of the forty-nine states, plus one for Washington, DC, I now was going to run out of Bibles before I got to Alaska.

It's interesting that the one stop that I talked about CMA the most on is the stop that caused me to run short of my CMA Bibles. However, the next day, I was on the phone to my brother in Christ, Ray Burns. Ray and his wife, Marian, are honorary members of our CMA Chapter, Heaven on Wheels, in Topeka, Kansas. Ray also serves on the National Board of Directors for CMA. Ray and Marian have served CMA in every way possible since the mid-1980s. I also knew that Ray and Marian had just been at Iron Mountain, the CMA International Headquarters, for our national rally. I called Ray because I knew he would have a supply of Hope for the Highway Bibles. Since I was going to be coming through Topeka the next day, Ray and Marian were thrilled to be able to meet up with me and restock my supply of Bibles.

When I was planning the trip initially, my plan was to drop into Kansas on Highway 75 coming down from Auburn, Nebraska, to Sabetha, Kansas. At Sabetha, I would get on Highway 36 and head west to Denver, Colorado. I knew that coming back to Topeka and taking I-70 west would probably be faster, but I was really very concerned about how I would handle being that close to home on day 5 of the trip. Would I have the ambition to keep going? Would I be so tired and lonely by that point that I would just decide to be done?

However, I was also riding a brand-new 2016 Harley-Davidson Road King that had just gotten its five-thousand-mile service two days before I left on the trip. I knew I was going to be putting almost twelve thousand miles on the bike in the two weeks of the total trip, but since they were all highway miles and it was only two weeks, I wasn't concerned about making the entire trip without a service on the bike. When I was talking to Mike Patterson, the owner of Historic Harley-Davidson of Topeka, where Jan and I purchase and service our motorcycles, he *totally* discouraged me on that idea. He told me that he would love to provide the midtrip service for me as his way of sponsoring the trip. *Wow!*

I arrived back in Topeka around 1:00 PM on day 5. Mike had two techs waiting for my Road King. It was in the shop immediately, no waiting in line. They treated my service like they were a pit crew for a race. They completely serviced the bike *and* put two new tires on. This service would normally be about a six-hour appointment and cost me about $1,000. They had me in and out in two hours. Besides my daughter-in-law in New York, Mike Patterson is the only other person that I specifically sought out to give a Bible to. While my bike was in his shop, I went to Mike's office, thanked him for his incredible generosity, presented him with a Bible, and prayed with him. It was unbelievably emotional and moving. I will never forget it. Thank you, Mike Patterson, for all the ways that you have supported and believed in Jan and me over the years. You're a great brother in Christ.

Again, God was demonstrating His wisdom is infinitely greater than mine. *My* plan was to stay away from Topeka. If I had followed my plan, I would not have been able to restock my Bible supply. *And* I would have missed out on the incredible blessing that I just talked about with Mike and his team at Historic Harley-Davidson. I tend to be very bullheaded and very confident in my own abilities (my wife and kids are screaming right now that I am understating by a mile). But here I was, halfway through my bucket list trip of a lifetime, seeing my loved ones temper their excitement in order to not tempt me to terminate the trip, and beginning to realize just how awesome our God really is. I was beginning to realize that He really does want us to enjoy our journey here on this earth. Seeking His will doesn't mean we will never have any more fun. In fact, I was beginning to understand that only through seeking His will, will we ever truly experience the fullness this life can offer.

CHAPTER 7
THE FINAL PUSH

Kissing my wife goodbye for the second time in five days and pulling away from Harley Town for the second time in six days were very different experiences from what I had felt at the beginning of the trip. The beginning of the trip was very emotional and a little bit scary as I was stepping into a journey with absolutely no experience. Now I was over five thousand miles into this journey and had already experienced a ton. Make no question, this second exit was definitely emotional, but there was a completely new level of confidence, not only in my own abilities, but I was beginning to understand and trust that God's planning was working out way better than my planning.

Before I move on ahead to the final push, I need to back up just a few hours. Another one of my good friends from CMA, Marv "Marvman" Ferguson, from Olathe, Kansas, had reached out to me a few weeks before the ride started to see if there was any point that I would be close enough for him to meet up with me and ride a ways. I was blown away that someone would want to do that and totally excited at the prospects.

In looking at the route and trying to estimate the timing, literally three or four weeks before the trip even started, we felt like he could meet me at my Missouri stop, which would be Rock Port. Rock Port is in the *very* northwest corner of Missouri, right at the intersection of I-29 and Highway 136. I was coming down I-29, having left Wahpeton, North Dakota, about 4:00 a.m. on day 5. I was communicating with Marv on day 4 to let him know that I was going to be on schedule and hopefully make it to Rock Port before lunchtime. Since I woke up early, probably because I was excited to get back to Topeka, I knew I would get to Rock Port before lunch. I got there about 11:00 a.m., and there was Marv waiting on me and ready to go. I filled my gas tank, and we headed west on 136 toward Auburn, Nebraska.

Marv rode right on my right hip all the way back to Topeka. When we pulled into Harley Town, the welcoming committee was all over me, and I was focused on getting the Road King into the shop. Marv just stood in the background and took it all in. I really felt bad that Marv had taken so much time out of his life to ride with me and we hardly got to talk at all. Some of that is just inherent with the fact that we were riding motorcycles and there is never much talking when you're riding, just by the nature of how you're traveling. But even when we got back to Harley Town, everything was such a whirlwind that I literally did not get to spend any time with Marv. Marv, I will *always* remember what you did, and these words do not even come close to expressing the appreciation I feel toward you. I love you, brother, and I thank you for riding with me.

In the afternoon of day 6, I was headed west on I-40, which parallels Old Route 66, through New Mexico. I had fueled in Albuquerque and was basically needing to stop for gas about every 175 unless a required stop shorted the leg. No required stops after Albuquerque, so I was just making great time. I started seeing bill-boards for what appeared to be a *huge* truck stop up ahead. Looking at the distance to the truck stop and my distance to empty gauge on the Road King, that truck stop was going to be perfect.

I don't remember why I called our CMA area rep, Brian Adcock, but I called him and we were chatting up a storm apparently. The next thing I know, I was looking up and noticing that I just went right by the exit for the truck stop. I still have a few miles left in the gas tank, so no problem, right? Also, I was carrying two one-gallon cans of gas with me, just for this kind of emergency. But quite frankly, I was carrying the extra gas more because I wasn't sure how far it would be between gas stations in Canada. I wasn't too worried about the good ole USA. Plus, I was sure I didn't want the embarrassment of running out of gas because of driving right past a truck stop that was being advertised for the last one hundred miles. I'm sure there'll be another gas station shortly anyway.

Just as my distance to empty gauge hit *zero*, I saw an exit with a gas station. I got off the exit, pulled up the station, only to discover it was *closed!* If I had been smart, I would have gotten my spare gas out and used it right then, because there was no traffic passing by to laugh at me. Quite frankly, it didn't even enter my mind at that point to use my spare gas. So back out on the interstate, just praying that a station with gas would suddenly appear. I had never tested to see how far past *zero* I could go before I actually ran out of gas, so I was really in uncharted territory. Ultimately, I did make it to the next gas station. When I pulled up to the pump, I even sat there for a minute with the bike still running, waiting for it to run out of gas. I finally shut it off. I put 5.8 gallons in a 5.3 gallon tank. How does that happen?

After I filled my gas tank, I went inside to get a snack and something to drink. As I was walking up to the entrance, I heard a voice behind me, "Hey, I like your patch." I turned around to see a gentleman about my age who seemed to be traveling with his family. We struck up a conversation, and it turns out he was a pastor from Joplin, Missouri, and we knew some of the same people. As we were talking, another gentleman standing in line just a few feet away said, "So you're from Topeka? I'm from Lawrence." Lawrence is just twenty miles from Topeka. This man was an over-the-road truck driver.

If I had followed my plan, I would have stopped for gas back at the big truck stop and never got a chance to meet these two gentlemen. By my calculations, there was no way I could have made it to that gas station. But I know that God knew and the God who made all creation, including the air I breathe, provided enough gas for my Road King to get to the station at just the right time to meet up with two of my neighbors, 1,500 miles from home.

Arriving in Umatilla, Oregon, was another huge rush. Umatilla, Oregon, was the completion of the forty-eight-states portion of the ride. I arrived in Umatilla at 1:00 PM PDT on day 8. It had taken me seven days, six hours to travel the 7,511 miles to complete this portion of the journey. *Wow!* I had just touched every one of the forty-eight states that make up our continental United States. I took a couple of selfies and took a picture of the receipt. These were some of the very few pictures I took during the trip itself, but I just couldn't help myself at this point.

Apparently, Oregon is like a few other states that don't do self-service at the gas stations. A young man that put the gas in the Road King for me was an obvious target for my last Bible before I headed to Alaska. But as I have said before, I didn't always want to settle for the obvious choice. So I went inside the store to purchase a snack and drink and to see who else might be in the store that I should be talking to. There were actually several people in the store, but I didn't get a sense that any of them was the one I was supposed to be talking to.

When I went back outside, the pump attendant was busy with other customers, so I just stood beside my bike until things slowed down for him. When he got a little break in the action, he actually approached me and wanted to hear a little more about the trip. The door flung wide open. I shared with him about giving away Bibles and praying with people along the way. When I asked him what I could pray for him about, he immediately mentioned his twin brother who was battling cancer. We prayed, and this young man is one of the few people that I met along the way who has actually reached out to me since the trip. This was an incredible divine appointment to complete this portion of the journey. Thank you, Jesus!

Day 9 was definitely the final push to finish the trip and get to Hyder, Alaska. About nine-thirty-ish that Sunday morning, July 3, 2016, I'm riding north on Highway 97 in British Columbia, Canada. This stretch of road is also called Cariboo Highway. I think it is absolutely breathtaking scenery, when you can see it. It was cold and raining. Temperature was in the mid-to-upper forties, and it has started raining around 5:30 a.m. I had been riding in rain ever since. I had stopped in a little town called 100 Mile House for gas just before 7:00 a.m. Since then I had also gotten past 150 Mile House.

The names of these towns were particularly interesting to me because distance in Canada is measured using the metric system of meters and kilometers, not miles.

Anyway, thinking about kilometers versus miles was keeping me occupied as I struggled to keep from freezing to death running off the road because I couldn't see through my foggy visor. About an hour or so, south of Prince George, British Columbia, I came up behind another motorcycle. Who else could possibly be as crazy as me to be out there on a motorcycle on a day like this? I followed for a few miles, excuse me, a few kilometers and then decided I could see well enough to pass. We waved at each other as I passed him, and I felt like he might even try to keep up with me leading the way, but he dropped back.

I got to Prince George and pulled in at the first gas station I saw. At first I thought the price of gas in Canada was ridiculously cheap. Then I realized their measure was liters, not gallons. That made the price of their gas about 25 percent higher than what I had been paying the rest of the trip across the USA. Anyway, I gassed up the Road King with their liquid gold and then went inside for some hot chocolate and warm air. I was not really ready to head back into the elements yet but knew I needed to keep pushing. Just as I was getting ready to mount my bike, the motorcycle I had passed an hour ago came rolling into the station. I had just given back all the time I had made up by passing him.

Turns out the guy was from Australia. He had his motorcycle shipped to Seattle. He had left from Seattle the day before and was headed to Prudhoe Bay, Alaska, to visit his son. Now *that's* a motorcycle ride. We actually talked for several minutes. I shared with him what I was doing, gave him a Bible, and was able to pray for him right there at the gas station. Once again, it was totally amazing how God orchestrated a guy from Kansas meeting a guy from Australia in Prince George, British Columbia.

I entitled this chapter "The Final Push," but I began the chapter talking about Marv riding with me immediately before I began "The

Final Push." So it only seems fitting to finish the chapter by talking about the last Bible, which happened the day after I arrived in Hyder.

As mentioned earlier, I arrived in Hyder about 6:30 p.m. PDT on Sunday, July 3, 2016. That was very close to the planned arrival time from the very beginning of the planning. I had reserved two nights at the Sealaska Inn and planned to spend the Fourth of July celebrating however they do it in Hyder.

I fell asleep early on the night I arrived and woke up at my usual 4:00 a.m. I went outside and walked around a bit, just taking in the unbelievable beauty that surrounded me. It was still a little hazy, but not nearly as foggy as it had been the day before. Since it was two hours later at home, I was able to call Jan and actually talk to her for more than just a minute or two. I talked to several of my friends and family that had been tracking throughout the entire trip. It was a great time of refreshing and celebration. I was overwhelmed as I considered the reality of what I had just experienced over the previous nine days. I don't know that I have ever felt the presence of God more clearly. It was an awesome few hours.

Toward the end of my solitude, I began a stroll down the main street of Hyder. Hyder states its population is at seventy-three. Most of the building along the main street are abandoned at best and basically falling down for the most part.

As I walked onto the main street, a typical American family, Mom and Dad and little Billy and Suzie, was coming onto the same street from the opposite direction. Now, we were walking together; actually, more accurately, we were standing together in the middle of the main street of Hyder, Alaska. Our introductions revealed that my new friends were from Chicago, Illinois, and had come to Hyder for a family reunion. In fact, they were going to be riding on their family's float that afternoon in the parade. We talked for a few minutes. We watched a black bear mosey across the street just about a half block away from us. I gave the dad my last copy of the New Testament Bibles that I have been giving out throughout my trip. And then we went our separate ways.

I ended up helping another couple set up their canopy for their hot dog and cinnamon roll stand. Turns out the wife is famous in that area for her cinnamon rolls, and because I helped them set up their booth, she gave me a couple of cinnamon rolls, which are the closest I've ever had to competing with the cinnamon rolls my mom used to make. They also explained to me about the event that was beginning to unfold that day. For us in the USA, we obviously celebrate Independence Day on the Fourth of July. Canada Day is celebrated on July 1 in Canada. Since Hyder, Alaska, and Stewart, British Columbia, are only separated by an imaginary line, marked by a bronze monument, the two cities join together each year for a four-day celebration they call International Days. The first two days of the celebration are in Stewart, and then the next two days of the celebration are in Hyder.

I didn't see any fireworks displays, but the celebration would rival anything I have ever seen in the continental US. There were some real pros competing in the axe-throwing contest. And let me tell you, the Nineteenth Annual Bush Woman Classic was the most competitive and entertaining event anyone would ever witness. And of course, the big parade. I couldn't help but marvel at the fact that in Kansas, most people are wearing as little as possible as they try to keep cool under the hot July sun. In Alaska, most of the spectators and even participants were wearing at least long sleeves, if not a jacket. Some were even wearing a stocking hat, and I saw a few hands being kept warm with gloves. Yes, quite a different experience for a Fourth of July celebration.

We were just a few minutes from the beginning of the parade, and I was milling around the hub of the activities when I heard my name called out from across the street. I turned around to see the dad from the family I had met on the street earlier that morning. He was striding toward me with a sense of purpose. He said that he had read the letter that I included in the Bible that I had given him and wanted to let me know that this was a really neat thing that I was doing. He asked me several questions about my family, life, and occupation back in Kansas. What really impressed him was that

I mentioned in the letter that I believed each person that I talked to on the journey was a divine appointment orchestrated by God. When I got the opportunity, I asked him about his occupation back in Chicago. He said, "I'm a rabbi." He gave me a wry smile since it was a New Testament that I had given him. I replied awkwardly, "Oh, so you're going to add that to the rest of your collections of New Testaments?"

He began to explain that he had several members of his synagogue that were Messianic Jews. He wanted to know if I knew that term. I explained to him that I not only knew the term but also had a friend who had grown up as a Jew and as a young adult converted to Christianity. Because of him, I also subscribed to an email published by a Messianic Jew. I finished my explanation by asking him if he was a Messianic Jew. He was almost apologetic as he explained that he had just not been able to get to that point yet. He believed Jesus was a great prophet, but he was not yet ready to accept the fact that He was the Messiah.

As we went our separate ways this time, I wasn't so sure that maybe this entire trip was just to meet my new friend, the rabbi from Chicago, on the streets of Hyder, Alaska. The rabbi is also one of the few that I talked to on the trip that has continued to communicate with me since the trip. We communicate via Facebook Messenger. A few months after I got home from the trip, I got a message from him. He always reminds who he is and how I know him, even though I pray for him and think about him all the time. In the message he said, "You remember that New Testament Bible you gave me in Hyder, Alaska? I just wanted you to know, it's all dog-eared now." He has never professed to becoming a follower of Jesus Christ, but I know the Lord is really working on him. One of these days, Jan and I are going to ride our motorcycles to Chicago and visit his synagogue. In the meantime, I continue to pray for my friend and am excited to see what God will do, in His perfect timing.

CHAPTER 8

CONCLUSION

I was on about day 3 or 4 or the ride when I knew that I needed to somehow capture all the experiences, thoughts, and blessings that saturated me throughout the fourteen days and nearly twelve thousand total miles of the trip. I had no idea what the book would look like, and I still don't know if what I've written captures the spirit of the journey for anyone other than myself. I pray that you have been inspired to look more diligently for the many ways God is working in your life, every minute of every day, and that you may realize that God truly delights in your pleasures.

Trying to figure out how to conclude this book very much reminds me of the very early morning hours of July 5, 2016. That was the appointed time, according to my plan, that I was to leave Hyder, Alaska, to begin the 2,550-mile trip home to Kansas. That was unmistakably the toughest day of the entire fourteen-day trip. I was confused. I was frustrated. Why was I so unmotivated to begin my trip home? I should be excited to begin my trip home. I knew Jan and many other friends and family were anxiously awaiting my arrival back home in a couple of days. I should be excited about that, right? But I was far from excited.

I was out of bed and ready to roll shortly after 3:00 a.m. on that Tuesday morning. I went through border patrol around three thirty and began making the forty-mile trip through the river valley and back to the highway that would take me 130 miles back south to New Hazelton, British Columbia, where I would pick up Highway

16, which is also the Trans-Canadien Byway. I wasn't even to New Hazelton yet when it started raining again.

Throughout the official ride, I had encountered every kind of weather imaginable for that time of the year, from one-hundred-plus-degree heat, to hurricane force winds (or so it seemed to me), to flash floods, to torrential downpour of rain, to steady drizzle, as we call it in Kansas combined with ridiculously cold temperature, especially given the time of year. During the official part of the trip, I had the adrenaline of the trip itself, the thrill of the competition of trying to prove myself physically and mentally capable of completing such a challenge to keep me going. I had completed that challenge about thirty-six hours ago. The adrenaline was gone. The thrill of the competition was over. Now, the only thing that was going to keep me going was the pursuit of completing the journey 100 percent.

It was about noon that day when I made it back to Prince George. My original plan for the return trip was to stay up in Canada all the way to Winnipeg, where I would essentially get on I-29 and take that all the way home. But as I have said before, I was really getting sick and tired of being cold and wet. My first chance to really head back south again was going to be at Prince George. As I approached Prince George, I was looking at the sky and for signs of improving weather. If I didn't see any improvement, I was going to head south at Prince George and follow the same route I had come up on to get back to the US and hopefully warmer weather just as quickly as possible.

Just as I was getting to Prince George, I began to see clearing skies to the east. As I approached the junction where I would either bail out and head south or stay in Canada, I felt the weather was improving enough to stay in Canada and see some more of our neighboring friends' land. By the time I stopped for gas and a lunchtime snack just east of Prince George, the sun was shining and the clouds were moving out. It wasn't very warm yet, but the sunshine helped a ton.

It was midafternoon when I was able to finally take off all my cold-weather clothing and act like it was July. By then, I was just entering the Jasper National Park in Alberta, Canada. I felt like I had been riding forever heading east, but when you look at the map, Jasper is basically straight north of Yellowstone. I was so glad I had stayed with the original plan. I don't know if I'll ever make it back up to Jasper again, but I was eternally grateful that I at least got to experience it this one time. And the weather could not have been more perfect, allowing breathtaking views over and over, with each passing mile (excuse me, with each passing kilometer).

Once I got past Jasper National Park and I was no longer wet and cold, I began to hear the siren call from home. Now I was once again focused on a goal. Now I was riding with purpose. I was headed for home, and there was no way I was going to get there fast enough.

As I've thought about this first day of the trip home in the months since the trip was completed, I am reminded that what I experienced was a lot like what many of us experience in our Christian walk. When we first come to know Christ, we are highly motivated. Each day is a new experience in the new journey we call Christianity. We are disciplined and passionate about our journey. We are learning and growing every day, and we're excited to share our journey with everyone around us. And then, one day, we wake up and realize that passion and motivation is just not what it used to be. Our discipline to do the daily tasks of being a "good Christian" seems to have disappeared as well. Maybe the rejection we have been experiencing from some of our so-called "friends" has begun to weigh us down. You start to feel sick and tired of being "cold and wet."

I am so glad that I didn't let my lack of motivation keep me holed up in Hyder, Alaska. As much as I enjoyed my brief time in Hyder, I'm quite certain my wife would not have understood one bit if I had told her I just didn't feel like getting back on the motorcycle right now. Maybe when it warms up a little bit and the sun starts shining, I'll see if I can get headed back then.

God revealed so many things to me during the fourteen days of this trip. He started revealing His will to me before the trip began, and He has continued to teach me lessons, as I reflect back on the trip, even today. I know very few people will ever have the opportunity or, for that matter, even the desire to do what I did in late June and early July of 2016. But God is working in all our lives each and every day, in whatever our circumstances and wherever we live. When the idea of doing this trip was planted in my consciousness, there was no thought of God in it all. It was purely a selfish "bucket list" experience for me. Even in my selfishness, God revealed Himself. Even in my selfishness, God used me. Even in my selfishness, God allowed me to pursue my experience. God turned the pride of having an Iron Butt into a Melted Heart.

I'm not worried about what God might ask me to do next. After this experience, I'm confident that if He has more He wants me to do, I'm ready and willing. One of my all-time favorite songs is entitled "Here Am I, Send Me!" I sing this song frequently at CMA rallies and such. In the words of the bridge, it says, "I will not fear what lies ahead, if you are by my side. I'll follow down the winding path if you will be my guide. Here am I, send me. Send me."

June 25-July 3, 2016

Dear Friend;

My name is Marshall Madill. I am from Overbrook, KS, about 60 miles west of Kansas City. I have been planning this trip that has now allowed our paths to cross for over a year. I have been dreaming about riding my motorcycle to Alaska since I was a youth. This particular trip is a lot more than just riding my motorcycle to Alaska. As you can see from the map below, I am currently in the midst of a ride that will take me through all 48 contingent states, Washington D.C. and finally to Alaska. This is the ride of a lifetime and I am truly blessed in SO MANY ways to be able to be making this journey.

As I was preparing for this ride, I also asked God to show me how He could use me throughout the trip. As you might suspect from looking at the map and comparing it to the dates on this letter, I am spending some very long days on my motorcycle each and every day of this trip. No sight-seeing. No joy-riding. No tourist stuff. Just trying to get another 1,000 miles down the road each and every day.

But, one of the things that I must do is stop in each and every state to purchase something in order to get a Time/Date Stamped receipt with the address to prove I was there. God impressed on my heart that I could take the time at each one of these stops to speak to one person and let that person know that God loves them. Hopefully this Bible will also help you to hear from God in a way that you've never experienced before.

This Bible is from Christian Motorcyclists Association (CMA). My wife, Jan & I are active members of Chapter 48, Heaven On Wheels in Topeka, KS. We love riding motorcycles and we love sharing the love of Jesus Christ wherever we go. I know it was probably strange when I started talking to you, but I have been praying about that moment for months. I believe God put us both in the same place at the same time for a reason. My phone # and email address are at the bottom of this letter. We also have CMA Chapters right here close to where you live. If I can help you in any way, please give me a call or email and I will do my best.

It was a pleasure speaking with you and I will continue to pray for you. May God's grace and the peace that passes all understanding be with you now and forevermore.

God Bless,

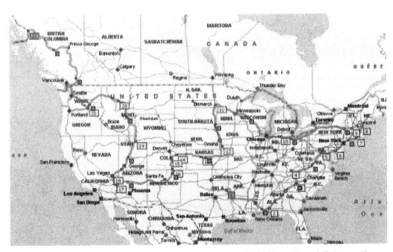

PHONE: (785) 248-6509   **EMAIL: mlmadill@gmail.com**

Just a couple of days before the beginning of the ride, I completed putting together the Bibles by signing all fifty letters and then placing a copy of the letter and the Jesus Film app in each Bible.

Fifty Bibles all ready to go, sitting patiently on my living room floor.

I had never owned a passport in my life. The day it arrived was a *very* exciting day for me as it was just one more tangible piece of evidence that this trip was *really* about to happen.

Final check of the gear on the last night at home in the picture above and on the morning of the official departure from our hotel in Idabel, OK, below.

2012 MTF 48+ Witness Form

Rider Name: _____   Motorcycle License # _____

Motorcycle Make/Model: _____   License State: _____

Begin Witness

Local Time: _4:50 AM_

Odometer: _5391_

Location Address: _Shell Station_

Idabell, OK

_____

If you're not using an MTF witness, IBA certified witness, policeman, firefighter, judge or notary public, you will need two witnesses!

Witness One

Name & Address: _[signature]_

Phone Number: _580-286-7021_

Signature: _[signature]_

Witness Two

Name & Address: _M Madill_

Phone Number: _785 845 9704_

Signature: _M Madill_

End Witness

Local Time: _6:49 pm_

Odometer: _14,120_

Location Address: _1001 Premier Ave_

The Sealaska Inn

Hyder, AK   99923

[signature]

If you're not using an MTF witness, IBA certified witness, policeman, firefighter, judge or notary public, you will need two witnesses!

Witness One

Name & Address: _____

Phone Number: _____

Signature: _____

Witness Two

Name & Address: _____

Phone Number: _____

Signature: _____

My official witness form. Once I made the decision to certify the ride, this witness form caused me the most stress of any other part of the planning. There are actual certified witnesses for Iron Butt rides. I reached out to a couple of certified witnesses that lived relatively close to Idabel, Oklahoma. They both told me not to worry about it. As long as I got two witnesses, I would be fine. They said that Jan could be one of the witnesses, so we were off to Idabel. Devontea was the attendant on duty at the Shell station that morning, so he got to be the other witness. What a great way to begin the ride!

My first official receipt above, from our motel in Idabel, Oklahoma. Notice the time stamp.

Below is the receipt from Umatilla, Oregon, which completed the forty-eight-states portion of the ride. Again, notice the time stamp. I began in the Central Time Zone and finished in the Pacific Time Zone. The official time for the completion of the forty-eight states was *seven days* plus *ten hours*.

2012 MTF 48+ Ride Log

Date	Time In (Local)	Time Out (Local)	Location	Odometer
3/25	4:	5:00 A	Isabell OK Deventea	5391
6/25		6:00	New Boston, TX Steve	5741
		6:50	Texarkana, AR Theo & Marty	5470
		8:15	Minden, LA Brian & Ruby	5569
		11:15	Jackson, MS Kevin & Girls	5762
		4:15	Century, FL	5999
		6:15	Montgomery, AL	6128
		10:00	Lawrenceville, GA	6318
6/26		3:45 A	Piedmont, SC —Ellen	6415
		5:30 A	Ashville, NC Greg/wife/Phillip	6493
		6:45 A	Johnson City, TN Austin/mom	6549
		7:15 A	Weber City, VA Val/Ronda	6575
		8:55 A	Pikeville, KY Larry + Mum	6665
		10:05 A	Stollings, WV	6228
		4:54 P	College Park, MD Andy	7125
		6:40 P	MIDDLETOWN, DE	7152
		8:25 P	North Hamilton Township, NJ	7301
6/27		6:50 A	Darien, CT GREG	7416
		8:30 A	Wyoming, RI	7523
		11:45	Salisbury, MA Madeline & Jason	7695
		12:45	Kittery, ME Ray Cortes	7715
		2:30	Hillsboro, NH	7797
		3:40	Brattleboro, VT — Will 17 yr-old	7845
		7:40	Canastota, NY Josh-Minnesota	8045
		10:55	Fredonia, NY	8258
6/28		5:30	Northern, PA FRED & Mark	8282
		7:50	Amherst, OH Denny - weight/A	8436
		10:45	Sturgis, MS GENO - Lois CHA	8616
		11:05	Howe, IN Carrie	8618
	CST	12:30	Chicago, IL John	8764
		4:10	Maustin, WI Cal & fiance	8970
		7:45	Rogers, MN Doug Allen	9193
6/29	10:15 P	4:10 a	Wahpeton, ND Darian	9373
		6:30	Brookings, SD Dan	9552
		8:50	Sloan, IA Gage & family	9692
		11:00	Rock Port, MO Randy Dot	9835
		11:35	Auburn, NE	9851
		5:10 P	Junction City, KS	10027
		2:25 P	Wakeeny, KS	10195

Page 1 of my official ride log

2012 MTF 48+ Ride Log

Date	Time In (Local)	Time Out (Local)	Location	Odometer
6/30		5:00 A	Cheyenne Wells	10348
		6:00 A	Kit Carson, CO	10400
		7:45 A	Ordway, CO Sesally & Braiden	10498
		10:40 A	Wagon Mound, NM — Brian Robb	10675
		1:15 P	Albequerque, NM Matthew	10851
		4:55 P	Holbrook, AZ Joplin & Topeka	11069
		7:30 P	Seligman, AZ	11240
7/1	PDT	8:45 P	Needles, CA	11374
		4:45 A		11375
		7:30 A	Henderson, NV Alberto	11472
	MDT	11:40 A	Cedar City, UT	11657
		2:30 P	Manti, UT Dalton, wrestler	11835
		4:45 P	Evanston, WY Alisa	11966
		6:30 P	Honeyville, UT	12072
		8:45 P	Idaho Falls, ID	12214
7/2	10:15 P	4:30 A	LIMA, MT	12313
		6:15 A	Butte, MT	12423
		11:15 A	Spokane, WA	12729
	PDT	1:00 P	Umatilla, OR David / Daniel	12902
		5:00 P	Omak, WA	13119
		7:00 P	Merrit, BC	13302
7/3	10:00 P	5:00 A	Kamloops, BC	13361
		6:55 A	100 Mile House, BC	13475
		10:30	Prince George, BC Paul / Australia	13679
		2:00 P	Houston, BC	13872
	6:30 P	3:45 P	New Hazelton, BC	13953
			HYDER, AK	14120

12402
5391
7511

Page 2 of my official ride log

The midway point in the ride, right back home in our office in Topeka, Kansas. While I was planning the trip, I was worried about coming back through Topeka for fear I would be tempted to just stop right then. Turned out to be one of the greatest blessings of the entire trip in three specific ways. Number *one*: Historic Harley-Davidson of Topeka did a complete service of my bike, including two new tires, at no charge. So I decided I wanted to give the owner of Historic Harley-Davidson, Mike Patterson, the Bible for Kansas. It was a very emotional exchange, which greatly touched both of us. Thank you, Mike Patterson. Number *two*: My good friends from CMA, Ray and Marian Burns, who are actually national directors for CMA, and

Carroll Fasse, were able to restock me more "Hope for the Highway" Bibles. I was giving away too many and would have run out if not for Ray and Marian sharing their supply with me. And number *three*: I got to see my beautiful wife for a few minutes. She kissed me and hugged me tight, in spite of the fact that I was in desperate need of a shower. With everyone stopping by to cheer me on and see how the trip was going, I didn't get that shower until very late that night in Cheyenne Wells, Colorado. Yes, it was just a bit difficult to kiss my wife goodbye for the second time in a week, but there was never a thought of stopping at this point. After two short hours, my bike was serviced, the Bibles restocked, and Jan sent me off with one of the best kisses of all time. Love you, babe!

I took this picture above with my camera. I *had* to take it because it is the exact same picture I saw on the internet when I was researching Hyder, Alaska. I had been looking forward to seeing this in person for more than a year. When I rounded the bend, this scene literally unfolded right before my eyes. What an *awesome* view to signal the finish line for my amazing journey and one I will definitely never forget.

Another hugely welcome sight was finding this little slice of paradise. The picture above was taken from the road looking back toward my room. My room was the first door to the right of my motorcycle.

The picture below was taken from the doorway to my room looking out across the road. These pictures were taken on July 4, 2016. Some of the snow just never goes away, but again, what an awesome sight!

The road leaving Hyder. The port of entry is actually in Canada. Notice the Canadian flag.

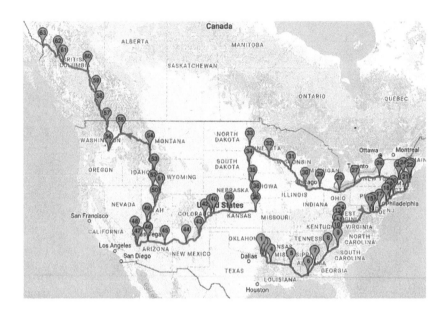

The route that was a part of the letter in each Bible was the planned route that I had found on the Iron Butt website. This route was created by plugging in the addresses from the receipts at each and every stop I made during the actual trip. Sixty-three stops, including the start and finish, 8,620 miles for the official ride. I added another 2,550 miles on the ride home.

THE REUNION ON I-29

I think I'm still in shock here. I'm pretty sure I've got tears running down my face.

My awesome friends, Mike McClain (who also wrote the fore-word for this book) to my right and Chuck Bramhall to my left. Another friend, Ron Hedges, headed out with the pack but had to turn back due to mechanical issues.

All together again and ready for the final two-hundred-mile journey back to Topeka. I could not have ever imagined a more fitting end to this incredible journey. Thank you, Mike, Chuck, and Ron. And, Jan, I love you to Hyder and back!

I completed all the required paperwork and had it mailed to the Iron Butt headquarters in Chicago by the end of July. I had no idea what to expect, but after a couple of months of checking the mailbox every day, I kind of started thinking that maybe they weren't certifying this ride any longer. We were sitting in our living room, relaxing on the Saturday after Thanksgiving in 2016, nearly five months after the ride was completed, when an express mail package arrived. I was practically in tears as I sorted through all the items inside the package. One item after another proclaiming what an incredible feat I had accomplished. *Wow!* What an amazing tribute. Once again, my heart just melted at the thought that God would choose to use me in such an enormous mission. Thank you, Lord.

Iron Butt Association

48 States plus Alaska in less than 10 days!

This is to Certify that in June of 2016, Marshall Madill rode a 2016 Harley-Davidson Road King through the 48 contiguous United States of America, across western Canada, and on to Alaska in 8 days, 17 hours! Mr. Madill's stunning 8,620-mile journey started in Oklahoma and continued on to Florida, Maine, California, and Washington, twisting and turning to ride in each state before ending in Alaska!

48 States Plus! is an extreme ride designed for an extreme rider. This ride was conducted under very strict guidelines set forth by the Iron Butt Association. Only a handful of riders from around the world have managed to solve the challenges such a grueling ride involves.

Michael J. Kneebone

Michael J. Kneebone
President, The Iron Butt Association

ABOUT THE AUTHOR

Marshall Madill, along with his wife, Jan, owns and operates a successful independent insurance agency in Topeka, Kansas. They have four grown children and eight grandchildren. Marshall is an elder in his church. He and Jan are both active in the Christian Motorcyclists Association. They view their business as a front for the many ministry opportunities that come their way on a daily basis.

Marshall grew up in Chanute, Kansas. His hero growing up was his maternal grandfather, Paul Life, who was a pastor in every sense of the word. When Paul Life took a church, the church came to "life." Watching his grandpa instilled a keen sense of "living out your faith" in Marshall.

Marshall has also dealt with an enormous amount of self-confidence and competitive spirit throughout his life. Surrendering to the leading of the Holy Spirit is not something that has come easily to him. It was the competitive spirit and his self-confidence that motivated him to take on this journey, but it was the leading of the Holy Spirit that got him through the journey.

CPSIA information can be obtained
at www.ICGtesting.com
Printed in the USA
BVHW051154020921
615898BV00022B/579